WHEN MOUNTAIN MEN TRAPPED BEAVER

they were constantly in danger—danger of Indians, of ferocious wild animals, of possible death from starvation or thirst. These rugged fur trappers lived and worked in the Rocky Mountains in the 1830's. There, in a huge wilderness more than 1,000 miles west of America's frontier, they lived rough, hardy lives.

Although these mountain men usually trapped the beaver streams alone, they enjoyed the companionship of their fellow trappers around the evening campfire. They looked forward to their "rendezvous" held each July, when they not only traded furs for supplies, but also participated in enough rollicking fun to last throughout the year.

Trappers were always on the move, looking for new places to set their beaver traps. As they moved, they felt the thrill of discovery, for they were the first white men to see the rivers, valleys, and snow-covered mountains of the American West. They blazed trails and discovered routes that were used later by settlers moving westward.

This is one of the How They Lived Series, developed by Garrard to give meaning to the study of American history. Young people will find a deeper understanding and a more lasting appreciation of history and geography as they see life in the past through the eyes of those who lived it.

When Mountain Men
Trapped Beaver

When Mountain Men Trapped Beaver

BY RICHARD GLENDINNING

ILLUSTRATED BY CARY

GARRARD PUBLISHING COMPANY
CHAMPAIGN, ILLINOIS

To Sally——as before

Picture credits:

American History Division, New York Public Library: p. 64, 65
American Museum of Natural History, New York: p. 69
Bettmann Archive: p. 25
City Art Museum of St. Louis: p. 27
Culver Pictures: p. 40, 89, 91
Denver Public Library Western Collection: p. 41, 59, 82
Gilcrease Institute of History and Art, Tulsa, Oklahoma: p. 9, 10, 71, 76
Historical Pictures Service: p. 29, 34, 68, 90
Library of Congress: p. 20, 21, 23
Metropolitan Museum of Art, New York. Morris K. Jesup Fund: p. 19
Missouri Historical Society: p. 45
Northern Natural Gas Company Collection, Joslyn Museum, Omaha, Nebraska: p. 18, 46, 47, 54, 66, 72
Picture Collection, New York Public Library: p. 5, 38, 49, 62, 73
Rare Book Division, New York Public Library: p. 21, 28, 53
Remington Art Memorial, Ogdensburg, New York: p. 1, 22, 37
The Trapper's Guide by S. Newhouse (New York: Mason, Baker and Pratt, 1874): p. 51, 58, 70
Union League Club, New York and Frick Art Reference Library: p. 30
University of Notre Dame Art Gallery: p. 6

Endsheets: *Grand Canyon of the Yellowstone*
by Thomas Moran, Gilcrease Institute
of American History and Art, Tulsa.

Contents

1. Comanches Get a "Teach"

Leading their pack mules by rawhide tethers, the six men in buckskin rode quietly and in single file. Every member of the little band was on the alert for the first sign of danger. Loaded rifles rested at the ready across the saddle pommels. Keen eyes scanned the rolling land. Not all the Indians in the Far West were unfriendly. But the Comanches were— and this was Comanche territory!

At the head of the group was Kit Carson, called "Little Chief" by the Indians. His sandy hair came down to his shoulders and was a bold invitation to any savage looking for a fine scalp. Then came Joe Meek, a big and happy-go-lucky man. Third in line was Bill Mitchell. Bringing up the rear were three Delaware Indians who served as camp keepers.

The men were fur trappers. But they were better known by another name: mountain men. They were called this because they lived and worked in the Rocky Mountains where beaver were plentiful along the swift, cold streams.

On this day in the 1830's, however, they were crossing a treeless desert, heading for some mountains far beyond. Only low scrub and cactus could live in the sandy soil under their horses' feet. Although it was only midmorning, the sun was already blazing hot. Water was many miles away and the supply the men had with them was fearfully low.

Suddenly Kit Carson threw up a hand of warning. "Injuns," he said quietly. But his band of trappers had already spotted the savages topping a small rise a thousand feet ahead of them. It was a swarm of the dreaded Comanches. More and more Indians kept coming over the hill until they seemed to fill the entire landscape.

Savage Indian attacks led by braves like these were a constant threat to trappers.

"Must be two hundred of 'em," Joe Meek said. "Well, boys, let's give 'em a teach." He meant that he wanted to give the Comanches a lesson they would never forget.

Kit Carson thought swiftly. In this bare land, there were no rocks to duck behind, no trees to fight from. And his men needed some kind of protection.

"Kill the mules," Kit ordered. "Make a fort of 'em."

The men sprang from their mules and jerked their hunting knives from their belts. Quickly they slashed the throats of their mounts and their pack animals. When the mules dropped, the men dragged them into a circular fort. The trappers sprawled behind the barricade with their rifles ready for the attack that was already coming.

"Yi-yi-yi-yi-yi-yi! Yip-yip-yip-yip! Yi-yi-yi-yi-yi-yi!" the savages howled as they charged down upon the makeshift fort. Indians thought that the more noise they made in battle the braver they became and the surer of victory. Their blood-chilling war cry was like that of a huge pack of mad dogs.

This "mule fort" in a painting by E. C. Paxson is like the one in which Kit Carson fought.

"Stagger your fire now," Carson cautioned, although his men did not need to be reminded of that. None of them was anxious to lose his hair to a Comanche scalping knife.

Even a man as skilled with a rifle as Kit Carson needed twenty to thirty seconds to load his gun and get off an accurate shot. In that same time an Indian could shoot eight to ten arrows with his three-foot, sheepshorn bow. If all the mountain men's guns were emptied at the same time, it would be easy for the Comanches to rush in and wipe the trappers out. So the mountain men staggered their fire to make sure that there were always some guns ready to fire while others were being reloaded. The Delaware Indians were in the thick of the fight, too, making good use of their guns against the Comanches.

On came the Comanches, screaming their wild cry. They had to get within seventy-five yards to make sure kills with their arrows. But the guns of the trappers could kill at ranges greater than a hundred yards. A mountain man fired and an Indian toppled from his pony. Another shot rang out from behind the fort of mule flesh—and another rider went down. Then, just as the Comanches came within arrow

range, their horses caught the smell of the
mules' blood. They reared up in terror. Before
the Indians could control them, two more dead
Comanches lay on the ground. The remaining
savages wheeled and sped away.

"They'll be back," Joe Meek said. "Never
fear about that."

Now there came a breathing time for the
mountain men. Perhaps they used it to "tell"
each other their wills. No mountain man ever
liked to think that he might be killed. But
even the bravest sometimes had to admit that
the future looked a little clouded. When this

happened, each man would tell the others what he wanted done with his belongings. They also gave each other messages to be passed along to families and friends in the settlements more than a thousand miles away. Survivors were honor-bound to carry out the last wishes of the dead.

While Kit Carson's men waited for the next attack, they sipped some water. They were sure their supply wasn't going to hold out much longer, no matter how careful they were with it. This worried them more than another attack by the Comanches. A man could tighten his belt and get along pretty well without food for a long spell. But water was another matter. Without it, men went through tortures worse than anything the Comanches could think up.

Joe Meek knew this. In his journal he once reported: "The worst suffering I ever had was from thirst." He knew, too, that water would be needed more than ever today. The blazing sun had made an oven of the desert. The unsheltered men would be baked dry.

The Comanches suddenly appeared over the rise. The mountain men sighted down their rifles and braced themselves for the second attack. On came the Comanches, howling and

whooping. Guns fired, Indians dropped, arrows filled the air. Then, following their pattern, the savages retreated—but only to attack again. And again and again. The battle raged all day under the burning sun. The water was gone. Already their throats were dry and burning and their tongues were swelling.

By nightfall, forty-two Comanches lay dead in front of the fort. Not one of the six trappers had been so much as scratched, although the dead mules bristled like porcupines with all the arrows sticking in them.

"The Injuns won't attack at night," Kit said. "I reckon we'd best pull out come full dark."

14

The men knew they would have to escape on foot. Under cover of the black night they crept softly away from their strange fort and headed in the opposite direction from the Indians. They journeyed all through the night, running, staggering, stumbling, their bodies aching for want of water. Their tongues were swollen. Their lips were parched and cracked.

They covered over seventy miles before they found water and the relief it brought. Many men would not have lived through such a journey. But to the mountain men there was nothing unusual about it. Such adventures were a part of their regular life.

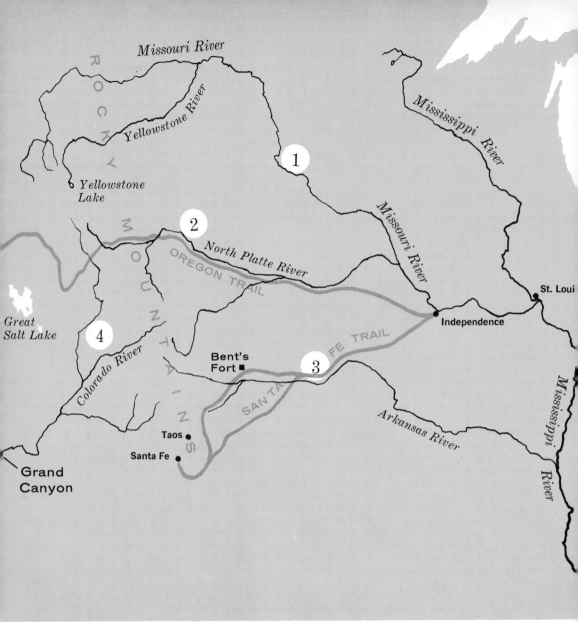

Missouri River

ROCKY

Yellowstone River

Yellowstone
Lake

Mississippi River

1

Missouri River

M
O
U
N
T
A
I
N
S

2

North Platte River

OREGON TRAIL

St. Loui

Independence

Great
Salt Lake

4

Colorado River

Bent's
Fort ■

3

SANTA FE TRAIL

SANTA

Taos ●

Santa Fe ●

Arkansas River

Mississippi River

Grand
Canyon

1. Keelboats carried trappers and fur traders up the treacherous Missouri River to the Rocky Mountains.

2. Other mountain men traveled westward by mule train on the Oregon Trail.

3. Huge Conestoga wagons carried men and merchandise southwest on the Santa Fe Trail.

4. Mountain men ranged far north and south in the Rocky Mountains in their search for beaver.

2. "You'll Do To Trap Beaver With"

In the 1830's, the Rocky Mountains of the Far West were a huge wilderness. They lay more than a thousand miles beyond America's frontier. Almost nothing was known about them in the East. Maps of that day showed mostly empty space for the Shining Mountains, as the Rockies were sometimes called. It was in that vast wilderness that the mountain men trapped beaver.

At that time fashionable men in the cities east of the Mississippi River, and in Europe, were wearing tall, black hats. Beaver fur made the best hats and beaver pelts brought good prices.

Some of the mountain men worked for large fur companies for regular wages. But many of them were free trappers. They worked only for themselves. They sold their furs to traders who came to a general meeting place once a year to buy the pelts. The traders made the long journey from St. Louis either by boat up the broad Missouri River or overland by mule train. They hauled in supplies and trade goods for the mountain men, and then took heavy loads of furs back to the East. The fur companies followed the same system.

But the yearly meeting of the trappers and traders was more than just a time to sell or

Karl Bodmer painted the wild fur trapping territory where the Missouri and Yellowstone Rivers meet.

Traders peacefully descend the Missouri with a pack
of furs in this G. C. Bingham painting.

buy pelts. To the trappers it was the high
point of the year. It was a noisy carnival that
lasted for weeks. They called it a rendezvous,
and looked forward to it eagerly.

There were probably never more than five
hundred mountain men working at any one
time in the wilderness. These few men were
spread over a million square miles of strange
land. It had some of everything. There were
terrible deserts. There were rich valleys car-
peted with wild flowers. There were tall peaks
where the snow stayed almost all year long.

There were broad plains that were the
grazing grounds for huge herds of buffalo.

Mountain men stand ready with their rifles watching
their leader advance to meet an Indian chief.

There were such wonders as the Grand Canyon,
carved by the Colorado River. And there were
roaring geysers and bubbling pools in what is
known to us as Yellowstone National Park. The
mountain men spent much of their time in
what are today the states of Montana, Idaho,
Utah, Wyoming, and Colorado. But the search
for beaver often took them even further west.

Their lives were in danger twenty-four hours
a day. When they went from place to place,
they kept a sharp eye out for trouble. They
scouted the land ahead as best they could.
Their horses and mules sometimes acted as
warning signals. At the first sniff of a fero-

cious grizzly bear, the frightened animals would cry out. But they could give little warning of a sudden attack by savage Indians.

Not all Indians were unfriendly. The mountain men traded with many tribes. Some of the men took Indian girls for wives and lived among their people. But tribes such as the Comanches and the Blackfeet were very hostile. They were always looking for the chance to take a white man's scalp.

Not even in camp could the mountain men feel safe from enemy redskins. When the trappers sat by a campfire, their trusty rifles were within easy reach. When they worked

A mountain man is introducing travelers in the West to friendly Indians.

A sandstorm surrounds Jedediah Smith and his men as they travel through the desert.

along a mountain stream, their guns were sure to be propped against a nearby tree. Just because there had been no recent sign of Indians did not mean that Indians weren't around. That famous mountain man, Jim Bridger, once put it this way: "Where there ain't no Indians, there you find them thickest!"

But Indians and wild animals were not the only risks the mountain men faced. There was starvation when game was scarce. There was death from thirst on the hot, dry deserts they sometimes had to cross. There was freezing in the howling blizzards that piled the snow deep in the mountain passes. There was the danger of drowning in the swift rivers. There was danger all around them as they went about their work.

Yet the trappers loved their way of life in the mountains. They loved the jagged peaks under a bright, blue sky. It was a land that gave them plenty of elbowroom. Mountain men hated to be hemmed in.

Old Bill Williams, a trapper who liked to travel alone, felt crowded if other trappers were working within ten miles of him.

"Ti-ya, now!" Old Bill would say in his odd way of talking. "This ol' horse is feeling all jammed up, an' that's fer sartain. Ay-e-e-e,

Indians walk into a trap set by these mountain men.

time's come fer this'un to be findin' hisself some breathin' space." And off he would ride.

The mountain men were alike in many ways but there were differences among them too. Some had had good educations. Some couldn't read or write. Jim Bridger was one of those. When he first went to the Far West he was not a free trapper. He worked for a fur company and had to sign the company's roster. He signed it with an "X".

Some mountain men were deeply religious, like Jedediah Smith, the great mountain man explorer, who carried his Bible everywhere.

This photograph of Jim Bridger was taken after he had become a scout for the Army.

But others did not know the meaning of prayer. Many of them were outlaws. They headed into the wilderness just in time to escape the sheriff.

But it didn't matter what a man had done before becoming a trapper. All that counted in the mountains was that he be loyal to his comrades. He had to be dependable when trouble brewed. That is why when one mountain man said to another, "You'll do to trap beaver with," he had more in mind than just setting traps in icy streams.

These men lived the simple life of Indians. But they had to beat the Indians at their own game just to stay alive. They had to be better woodsmen, better fighters, and better hunters. They had to be better and tougher in every way.

A mountain man never complained about hardships. That was part of his code. He never showed fear or pain. Always putting on his boldest face, he joked in battle and laughed at death. He did not let it bother him that at least one mountain man would die violently every ten days.

A hard life was a cheap price to pay for the right to be the first white men in that beautiful land. They were there to trap the beaver, but they were explorers too. They had the thrill of discovery. And they were helping to fill in the empty spaces on the maps.

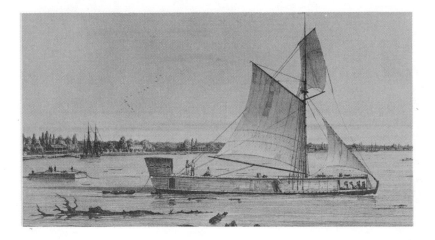

3. "I Took Ye fer an Injun"

There were two ways for the trappers to get from St. Louis on the frontier to the stronghold of the mountain men in the Rockies.

The first was by keelboat up the Missouri River to its headwaters 2,950 miles away in Montana. That was the way that such famous trappers as Jedediah Smith, Jim Bridger, and Tom "Broken Hand" Fitzpatrick made their first trip to the Far West.

The river route put the trappers in rich beaver country. But it was a hard journey. It was against the current all the way. Also the

Traveling by keelboat, trappers and traders camp for the night on the banks of the Missouri River.

"Big Muddy"—as the Missouri was often called —could be mean and tricky. Boats ran aground on sandbars. Changing currents and tangles of logs just below the surface tipped the boats over. Surprised men and valuable cargo were dumped into the water.

To make it even worse, sails were not always useful. The heavy boats had to be wrestled up the river by muscle power. Men pulled strongly on oars or used long poles to push against the river bottom and inch the craft upstream. Where the shore was level enough, they plodded along the bank with long ropes slung over their shoulders and towed the boats which were from sixty to seventy-five feet long.

And as if all that weren't enough, there were redskins along the way who did not want white men coming into their country. When Indian scouts spied a boat moving slowly up the river, they raced off to arouse their friends. Then the hostile savages swarmed to the river's edge. They crouched in hiding behind bushes and waited for the boat to come in sight. When it was within range, the Indians let fly a cloud of arrows. The boat made an easy target and many trappers died on their way up the Missouri.

Giant prairie schooners move slowly westward in this painting, *Ships of the Plains*, by Samuel Colman.

So it was that the second way to the Far West became the favorite path of trappers and traders. This was the overland route. Pack trains of mules took a route that became famous as the Oregon Trail. Then there was the Santa Fe Trail that went past Bent's Fort and on down into Mexican territory. Heavy, high-wheeled prairie schooners usually followed that route.

Kit Carson made his first trip to the West over the Santa Fe Trail. He was sixteen and small for his age. When he asked for work with a westbound wagon train, the captain of the train gave him the job of taking care of the extra animals. Kit had to drive his cavvy— as the mixed lot of horses, oxen, and mules was called—behind the wagons. It was a nasty job because there the dust was thickest. But Kit did not complain. He knew that greenhorns always got the meanest jobs.

Young Kit had probably seen mountain men when they made rare visits to the settlements in Missouri. But there the trappers would have been clean and wearing their finest buckskins. His first look at them in the Far West may

have been as he traveled with the wagon train along the trail to Bent's Fort. If trappers happened to be at the fort when wagons were approaching, they often rode out to meet them. When the howling mountain men galloped down upon the wagons, Kit may well have grabbed for his rifle. Many newcomers to the West did just that. They were afraid they were being attacked by Indians.

The mountain men thought this was a great joke and they made the most of it. Riding in

tight circles around the train, they fired their guns into the air and screamed blood-chilling cries. The greenhorns would finally see that these were really not wild Indians. Then they joined in the laughter.

But who could blame the tenderfeet for confusing mountain men with Indians? Even mountain men themselves did this. Frederic Remington, an artist famous for his paintings of the West, once drew a picture of two trappers meeting along a trail. They look

I Took Ye Fer an Injun by Frederic Remington.

enough alike to be twins. As they stare each other up and down, one says, "I took ye fer an Injun."

The mountain men wore their hair long, either hanging straight to their shoulders or braided in Indian style. Few trappers carried razors. Some let their beards grow long and tangled. Some shaved with their sharp hunting knives. And some others did as the Indians did. Either they singed their whiskers or they jerked them out hair by hair.

The trappers were like Indians in other ways. Most of them seldom bathed. The nearest to washing they ever came was when they accidentally fell into a stream. But there were some who stripped once in a while and scrubbed themselves clean with sand.

A mountain man spent no more time washing his clothes than he did himself. The smoke of many campfires was deep in his greasy buckskins. But the buckskins were greasy for a good reason and the greasier they were, the better. Grease made good weatherproofing. It helped keep out rain and the cutting winds of winter. That is why mountain men always wiped their greasy knives on their loose-fitting hunting shirts after each meal.

There were also good reasons for the deer-skin fringe on their shirts and breeches. It kept rain from seeping through the seams, and it gave the trappers a handy supply of leather strips. They used these to make repairs on such things as snowshoes and moccasins. When they were trapping beaver they wore buckskin pants that ended at the knees. Below that the trappers wore cloth leggings. And again there was a good reason for it. They set their traps as they waded in water, and leather would have shrunk and then tightened like bands around their legs.

The trapper usually wore a hat of wolf fur in the winter. And in summer he protected his head with a bright red or blue bandanna. In summer, too, his buckskin trousers might be replaced by the simple breechclout that the Indians wore. But winter or summer, he wore moccasins made of elk hide. The best skin for such shoes came from old Indian tepees. The smoke from the many fires built in the tepees made the hide extra tough. It also cured the leather so that it held its shape even when it was wet.

The trappers hardly ever stayed long in one place. They kept moving on in search of better

Trappers were prepared to move quickly and to fight
in open country as in this Remington painting.

beaver streams. Also they were always dodging
unfriendly Indians. So they carried little.

They took only what they needed on the
trail or at work. A hatchet, a hunting knife,
and perhaps a single-shot pistol were tucked
into the broad belt around a trapper's waist.
Over his shoulder he carried his powder horn
and his "possibles" sack. This was a leather
bag that held the things he might possibly
need: needles and thread, fish hooks, flint and
steel with which to start fires, pipe and tobacco,
and a few personal items. Over his shoulder,

37

His trusty rifle handy, a mountain man stops to let his pack mule drink from a quiet stream.

too, he carried his bullet pouch and perhaps a chunk of lead and a mold with which to make more bullets.

Every mountain man also carried a small bottle that held beaver "medicine." This was a mixture that each trapper invented for himself. Mountain men would give up their lives for each other but they seldom shared the secret of their medicine. This was a strong-smelling concoction made from beaver glands and different kinds of wild herbs. It was used to attract the beaver to the traps. Each trapper was sure that his bait was best, so he kept its secret to himself.

38

The most important thing that any trapper owned was his rifle. His life depended on it. But almost as important were his steel traps. Each man usually had six of them. They weighed between five and six pounds and cost fifteen dollars apiece. The trappers carefully guarded their traps; it was a long way to St. Louis for new ones.

Sometimes a trapper toted a cooking kettle with him. And sometimes he had a tin cup. But he seldom bothered with a fork or tin plate. Instead he ate from his hand or the point of his knife and used bark from a tree if he needed a plate.

With these few things and either a buffalo robe or a blanket capote—a kind of hooded cloak—to keep him warm, a mountain man was ready for the trail.

4. On the Trail

When mountain men made camp in the wilderness, they looked for three things: a water supply, grass for their horses and mules, and cover from hostile Indians. This usually meant setting up the camp near a spring or along a stream.

But grizzly bears liked the same places! The huge, ferocious beasts went into the thick undergrowth near the water to feast on the wild berries that grew there. Nothing was more to be feared than a powerful grizzly. The shaggy animal stood nine feet tall when he rose up on his hind feet. A full-grown grizzly might weigh as much as a thousand pounds. He was strong enough to break a horse's back with one swipe of his clawed paw.

Jedediah Smith once almost lost his life because of a grizzly. Jedediah was leading his men through a thick undergrowth. The trappers were on foot and moving in single file, leading their animals by their tethers. They were journeying to fresh trapping waters and were near a fork of the Cheyenne River. Jedediah's first warning of danger came when the mules screamed in fear and tried to bolt. He dashed back along the column to see what the trouble was. He came suddenly on a huge bear.

Jedediah threw his gun to his shoulder. But before he could pull the trigger, the red-eyed beast rushed at him and slapped the rifle from his hands.

Jedediah went to the ground under the crunching weight of the great bear. His side burned painfully as the grizzly's sharp claws raked him. Then the gray-brown monster closed his huge jaws around his head. Blood instantly filled the trapper's eyes. Still Jedediah struggled to defend himself. He managed to pull his hunting knife from his belt. He drove it into the grizzly's side. He stabbed again and again. It is not certain if the blade found the bear's heart or if one of Jedediah's men finally killed the big animal with a well-aimed bullet. But the grizzly died and strong hands rolled the heavy body from the wounded leader.

Three of Jedediah's ribs were broken. A deep wound slashed across his forehead from above his left eye. His scalp was badly torn. His left ear dangled loose. He was growing weak from loss of blood and he was in great pain. His men stared at him in horror. They had seen serious accidents before. But this had happened to their leader, the man who usually took charge in an emergency.

It was their leader who finally took charge of his own operation. First he sent men to the nearby river for water to wash his wounds. Then he looked up at Jim Clyman, a veteran mountain man. "You've got to sew me up, Jim," he said.

Jim nodded grimly. He knew nothing about doctoring but something had to be done. He hurried to his "possibles" sack and got scissors, a sewing needle, and ordinary thread. First he shaved Jedediah's head and stitched the scalp as best he could. Then he worked on the forehead wound. But he didn't know what to do about the dangling ear.

"Stick it back on the best you can," Jedediah ordered.

Clyman flattened the ear against the side of Jedediah's head and sewed it in place.

Then Jedediah was taken to the bank of the river, where camp was pitched. One of the trappers found a bit of soap. This was mixed with some precious sugar from the food stores and made into a salve for his wounds. Simple mixtures like this were the only medicines the trappers had. Some ailments called for salve, others for bitter teas made from berries, bark, and roots. But mountain men really had no need for fancy medicines. They almost never were sick.

After Jedediah's ribs were bound and his wounds dressed, he rested in a small tent. There he read his Bible and wrote in his diary. Within ten days he was able to travel and get back to his trapping. His quick recovery was because of his toughness and good condition.

Even though Jedediah was ready for the trail in only ten days, this was longer than the mountain men liked to stay in one camp if they were in dangerous country. Safety from unfriendly Indians lay in keeping on the move.

Unfriendly Indians attack a lone trapper in William Ranney's *Trapper's Last Shot.*

The trappers liked to set up their camp well before dark. Sometimes they would have two camps. At the first camp, they would build small fires. If there were any cottonwood trees nearby, they would use the branches and twigs because cottonwood gave off so little smoke. Then they would cook their evening meal, put out the fire and move on to a "cold camp" a mile or more away. There they bedded for the night, with no fire to tell hostile Indians where they were.

Even if they felt safe, they kept on guard in setting up a new camp. They hobbled their horses and mules with rawhide thongs to keep

One trapper tries to hobble a balky horse while his companions set up camp in this Miller painting.

Sleepy trappers, awakened during the night, try hard
to save their horses from Indian thieves.

the animals from wandering too far from
camp. Even friendly Indians would steal horses.
Horses were a sign of wealth among Indians.
And to steal a horse was counted as an act of
bravery. The Indians called this kind of daring
deed "counting coup."

After the animals were cared for, the camp
keepers fetched water and wood and made the
cooking fires. One fire would be enough for a
small party of four to eight trappers. But
large brigades of twenty—or even forty—men
would need a fire for each three or four men.
Each small group was known as a "mess." The
camp keepers were sometimes Indians. Often

47

they were white men who were newcomers to the mountains. They took care of the duller chores and remained behind to look after the camp while the veterans tended the traps. The traps were always set just before dusk. This was probably the time, too, that the camp keepers did the cooking.

The cooking was kept very simple. Sometimes there would be a stew made of buffalo meat or venison or rabbit and wild onions and turnips. Sometimes there would be game birds roasted over the fire or a deer's head baked under coals. Or there might be trout fresh from the nearby stream. Bread was rare. Jim Bridger once said he hadn't tasted bread for seventeen years and had lost all liking for it.

The coffee, more often than not, was made from acorns. Except for sugar, which was usually scarce, the only sweets were wild berries. In fact, the mountain man's diet was almost entirely meat. If it wasn't cooked over his fire, he ate it in sun-dried strips called "jerky" or in the form of pemmican. Pemmican was a mixture of buffalo meat, fat, and wild berries all pounded together. Packed into a leather bag, it kept for months and could be eaten in an emergency.

48

When there was no fish or game to be had, nor any pemmican for empty stomachs, mountain men ate roots. They even boiled their moccasins and belts, and then drank the broth to give them strength.

Yet no matter what they ate, they were as healthy as any band of men had ever been. Old Bill Williams claimed it was because of the buffalo meat in their diet. He said that it was the very finest medicine there ever was.

After the evening meal, the mountain men rested—but with their rifles ever ready. They took out their stone pipes and packed them

with tobacco. The mixtures they smoked were made from the leaves of the bearberry bush, from dogwood bark, from red cedar shavings, and from the small leaves of the wild tobacco plant when they could get some of it. While they smoked near the dying fire, they talked quietly of past adventures or they spun tall tales to delight each other. Sometimes, too, they used this time to repair traps or mend harness.

Then it was time to turn in after posting the night's watch. Sometimes they built small lean-tos of boughs and sometimes they had tents. But most often they slept under the stars, perhaps on a bed of balsam. With a buffalo robe or a Hudson's Bay blanket to keep off the chill, sleep came quickly.

Wolves howled on the distant ridges. The horses and mules stirred nervously. Tired trappers slept while guards kept watch.

5. "Beaver Medicine"

The trapper stood as still as a rock. Only his eyes moved as he peered through the bush and looked up and down the stream. It was nearing twilight and birds twittered in the trees as they settled for the night. If there were Indians moving nearby, the birds would be silent. The trapper watched the water for floating leaves or twigs. There were none. That was a fair sign that no one was standing on the bank further upstream—someone whose movement might have shaken the undergrowth.

For ten minutes the mountain man stood steady. Then, as sure as he could be that there

was no enemy about, he picked up a five-pound
trap. Slinging it over his shoulder by its five-
foot chain, he stepped into the icy stream. The
beaver dam lay thirty yards upstream. But
even without the dam, the trapper would have
known that beaver were here. He read the
signs clearly. He saw the gnawed branches of
the cottonwood and the basswood. These, with
the bark of the willow, birch, and aspen, were
favorite foods of the beaver. He saw the fallen
trees. He saw, too, the chutes the beaver made
when they slid down the muddy banks into the
pool behind their dam.

Beaver built their dome-shaped houses of mud and branches at the edge of the pool. The entrance to the lodge was an opening below water level and led through a tunnel to the inside of the house above. Beaver have very keen noses. That is why the trapper waded upstream to reach their houses. It cut down the chances of their catching his scent. The trapper chose a place near a beaver hole. He spread open the powerful jaws of the trap. Then he carefully placed the trap on the bottom of the pool in three to six inches of water.

The beaver hut and its tenants were painted by Karl Bodmer who traveled up the Missouri River in 1834.

Setting Traps for Beaver by Alfred Jacob Miller.

Next he stretched out the five-foot chain which had a ring at its end. He drove a pole through the ring and into the bottom of the stream to anchor the trap. Then he fastened a stick to the trap at the end of a long thong. Now, even if the beaver should drag the trap into deep water, the trapper could find it because of the floating stick.

Next he baited the trap. A few feet above it he stuck a four-inch stick into the muddy bank. Then, taking the bottle of his secret mixture or "beaver medicine" from his belt, he smeared some of the medicine on top of the stick. Old trappers claimed that the beaver could smell the lure a mile away. Drawn by the smell of the bait, the beaver would stand up on his hind feet to get at it. He would step into the trap and the steel jaws would snap around his leg. The trapper hoped that the beaver would then drown before he could gnaw his leg free.

Satisfied with the setting of the first trap, the mountain man waded downstream to set another. He set six traps in all. Then, with darkness coming on, he returned to camp. His fellow trappers were also coming into camp. Each of them had worked alone. They wanted

it that way. They shared dangers together but not trapping methods.

At the break of day, the mountain man returned to his traps. But he was as careful as he had been the night before to make sure no Indians were near. He was pleased to find that five beaver had taken his bait. That was a good night's catch.

He hauled the catch up on the bank and set to work with his sharp hunting knife. First he made a long slit down the belly of one of the beavers, then a slit inside each leg, and then he skinned it. These beaver were full-grown. They weighed more than thirty-five pounds. Their pelts weighed between one-and-a-half and two pounds each. Back in St. Louis the furs might bring as much as eight or ten dollars apiece. But the mountain man wouldn't get half that much money from the traders who bought them at the rendezvous.

Except for the pelts, all of the beaver that the trapper carried back to camp with him were the glands and the broad, flat tails. The glands he would use to make more medicine. The tails were good to eat when skinned and boiled.

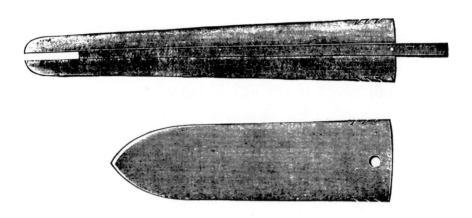

Board frames like these were often used in place of willow or hoop frames. The animal skins were pulled tightly over the stretcher and allowed to dry.

At camp, the pelts were scraped of flesh. Then the furs were stretched on willow frames and set out to dry in the sun. When they were dry, they were folded with the fur side in and packed sixty to eighty furs to a bale. Wet thongs of rawhide were wrapped around the pack. The thongs shrank when they dried and made tight, strong straps.

Naturally, the mountain men wanted to take as many beaver pelts as possible to the rendezvous. But the bales of fur caused a problem. Each one weighed close to a hundred pounds. If trapping was good, a party of trappers could soon make up more of the heavy bales

58

than their mules could carry. So they needed a place to store their furs while they moved on to other trapping grounds. It must be a place well hidden from the Indians. So they made a cache, or hiding place.

To make a cache, the mountain men first chose a mound near a stream. Into the side of the mound they dug a tunnel that soon widened into an underground room. All the earth they took out was put on a buffalo robe and carried to the water's edge. There it was dumped into the stream and swept away by the current. In this way no piles of earth were left near the cache to give the secret away.

Mountain men moving to new trapping grounds have no room on their mules for heavy bales of fur.

When the room was finished, it was lined
with poles and branches. The furs were tightly
packed into it and the hole in the side of the
mound was plugged. Then the trappers built
a campfire on top of the mound, which soon
burned out. To give the final touch to their
hiding place, the trappers let their animals
trample down the area. The hoof prints around
the cache, plus signs of the campfire, made the
place look like just another overnight stop
along the trail.

The mountain men had wonderful memories for places and would have no trouble finding the spot when they came back again. To help them, though, they picked out special landmarks like a lightning-struck tree or an oddly shaped rock.

But sometimes the hiding place was not safe. Indians discovered it and took the furs, or water seeped into it and ruined them. Then when the trappers returned for the valuable pelts, they found their hard work had been for nothing. But they soon forgot it. A man couldn't brood over trouble in the wilderness. Besides, there were always other beaver to trap. So the mountain men moved on to other streams.

6. Buffalo on the Plains

The sun was climbing into the morning sky as a party of mountain men prepared to break camp. The trappers were crossing the broad plains on their way to a stream that had not been trapped for some time. They hoped to find plenty of beaver there. The mules stood ready for loading and the saddled horses were hobbled a short distance away.

Suddenly a trapper rode furiously into camp. He had gone out earlier to scout the land. "Buffler!" he shouted. "Buffler comin' this way!"

All thought of breaking camp was now forgotten. The men had not tasted fresh buffalo meat for several weeks. The hunt was on!

Quickly they stripped themselves of any gear they would not need on the hunt. They tied bandannas around their heads to keep the hair out of their eyes. Snatching up their loaded rifles, they dashed for their horses. Even as they ran, they fumbled bullets from their pouches and popped the lead balls into their mouths. There they would be handy for reloading the guns. Eyes shone with excitement as the trappers vaulted up on their horses. There was nothing to match a buffalo hunt for thrills—not even a fight against Indians. A man's first buffalo hunt was something he never forgot.

The trappers galloped out of camp, topped a rise, and saw the herd of buffalo in the distance. Thousands of the huge, shaggy-headed beasts stretched as far as the eye could see. They had not yet caught the scent of the half-dozen hunters and were moving slowly, grazing on buffalo grass. Dust rose from their plodding feet in a thick cloud.

The hunters reined their mounts to a sudden stop. One of the men leaped from his horse and plucked a stem of grass from the ground. He tossed it into the air and watched it drift with the wind. This told him which way the wind

was coming from. The hunters rode against
the wind so that the herd would not smell
them and begin to stampede. To make a sure
kill, the mountain men had to ride close to the
buffalo's side and aim for the spine or lungs.

But the big beasts caught the man smell.
The herd began to run! The sound of thunder-
ing hooves was like the noise of an oncoming
storm. The cloud of dust grew thicker. The
hunters rode into it as they chased the buffalo.
Soon they were surrounded by stampeding
beasts. If a horse stumbled now on the rough
ground, its rider might fall and be trampled to
death under the pounding hooves. Yet the

daring hunters guided their horses only with
their knees! Their hands were free to use
their guns.

Each man picked out a fat cow and edged
alongside until his leg almost touched the
buffalo. Then he took careful aim just behind
the right shoulder. This was hard to do because
of the dust in his eyes and the wild motion of
his running horse. But a mountain man knew
how to handle his gun. He fired. The buffalo
stumbled and went down heavily.

Now the hunter had to reload while his horse
raced at full speed. He quickly dumped powder
down the muzzle and spat a bullet after it. He

seated the bullet by slamming the gun butt
down on his saddle. He poured more powder
from the horn into the firing pan. It wasn't
possible for him to measure carefully with his
horse plunging under him. So he put in extra
powder to make up for what would be spilled
in the wild ride and went after his second cow.

By the end of the hunt the mountain men
were as tired as their horses. But there was
more work to be done. The dead buffalo had
to be butchered. That meant first getting the
heavy animals—weighing almost as much as a
ton—up on their bellies, with their legs spread

Some Indians and a trapper prepare to butcher their
prize—a fallen buffalo.

out like braces to the sides. Sharp knives cut through tough hide along the spine. Then the skin was peeled down so the hunters could get at the meat underneath.

Veteran mountain men liked buffalo meat so much that they couldn't wait until they got back to camp for their first taste of the fresh kill. They cut out the liver and ate it raw, sometimes seasoning it with some gunpowder. A greenhorn usually wasn't quite up to that on his first hunt but he would take the tail of his first buffalo as a trophy.

There were few parts of the buffalo that a mountain man wouldn't eat. The tongue was tasty. So was the boss, or hump on the back of the buffalo's neck. The ribs, the fat, the bone marrow, the kidneys were all good. If meat was scarce, everything that could be eaten was taken back to camp. In time of plenty, the mountain men took only the best parts. The rest was left on the plains for the wolves.

What a feast there was in camp after a hunt! Each man usually built his own fire and did his own cooking. Some parts of the buffalo were boiled and others fried in buffalo fat. But most of the meat was roasted over the coals on the end of a ramrod or a green stick.

The men joked and laughed as the eating went on and on. They could stow away eight pounds at a sitting. Then they would fall over on their backs, rest a while, and come back to eat another eight pounds. Their hunting knives and hands were their only tableware. Their laps were their tables. By the time they were through, they were smeared with grease, blood, and juices. But they were wonderfully happy and they laughed at the sight of each other's smeared faces. None of them ever got sick from overeating.

Mountain men seldom kept the buffalo hides unless there were friendly squaws nearby to

Pieces of buffalo meat hang over the wagon tongues to dry while trappers feast on choice hump ribs.

scrape them and soften them. In the summer, when the body of the buffalo was almost bald, the hides were tanned by the women for tents and pouches. In the winter, when the buffalo's hair was thick, the hide was used for heavy clothing, blanket robes, and warm moccasins.

Nothing was more important to Indians and mountain men than the buffalo. The huge herds fed, clothed, and housed them. There were so many of these big animals on the plains that it seemed there could never be an end to buffalo hunts. But mountain men thought that about the beaver trade too.

7. "Rocky Mountain College"

Winter came early to the mountains. The trappers read the signs of it. Light snows began to fall on the lower slopes. Thin ice formed along the edges of the streams. Wildlife moved down from the high mountains into sheltered valleys. Soon it would be too cold to trap beaver. The time had come to get ready for winter.

To some mountain men, that meant saddling up their horses, packing their finest buckskins, and heading south. They headed for the village of Taos, in Spanish-Mexican territory. There they stayed until spring came and they could trap in the mountains again.

Men who had married Indian squaws often spent the winter in the warm tepees of their wives' people. Others waited through the cold and snowy days at such posts as Bent's Fort on the Santa Fe Trail. A very few made the long trip back to the settlements on the frontier. But most of the trappers lived in the mountains in winter lodges.

They carefully chose the places for these winter camps. First they wanted a valley protected from cold winds. They wanted a good supply of wood for cooking and heating. They

Fort Laramie shown in this Miller painting was the winter home of many trappers.

Lonely trappers often visited friendly Indians like
these Minnetarees in their snow-covered village.

wanted water. They wanted plenty of game for
food. They wanted a good stand of cottonwood
trees. Their bark made a good winter feed for
horses and mules. If a tribe of friendly Indians
was living nearby, so much the better. The
squaws could be put to work making some new
clothing for the mountain men. And also, the
Indians' camp was a good place to visit. It was
a change from the winter lodge.

The lodges that the trappers put up were
sometimes tepees of buffalo or elk hides. These
tepees were as tall as twenty feet and just as
big across. At the pointed top, where the poles
met, there was a hole to let out the smoke.

But often the trappers put up log cabins. These had no windows, and the floors were hard-packed dirt. The only light came from large, stone fireplaces. With so little ventilation, the cabins were usually smoky and smelly. Their only furniture was what the men made. Benches and tables were made from split logs. Beds, grouped along the sides of the room, were made of pine boughs. The men rolled up on them under their blankets and buffalo robes.

After the hard work of trapping in the fall, winter was almost a loafing time. But there were chores to be done. Each man had to peel

A huge grizzly bear surprises a mountain man at the door of his winter cabin.

enough cottonwood bark every day to feed two animals. Wood had to be cut and water carried. There were regular hunts to keep up the food supply. Then too, the mountain men usually set out traplines for wolves and other wild beasts, whose fur was valuable. Most of their time the men spent indoors near a roaring fire.

This was when they made new moccasins and other leather goods if there were no squaws handy to do that work for them. They mended their gear and put their precious traps in top shape. They spent their idle time play-

ing cards and dominoes and weaving tall tales.
Also, while they puffed on their willow-stemmed,
soft-stone pipes, they went to "Rocky Mountain
College."

Some men had brought books to the West.
They brought only the best ones because they
had to travel light. These books were read
aloud over and over again. Soon trappers who
could neither read nor write were able to recite
from the poems and plays of William Shake-
speare. They could also repeat verses of other
English poets. They learned about the gospel

from Bible readings. They learned about world history and geography from the educated men.

Along with what they called "book larnin'," they also learned each other's wild tales. Jim Bridger was rated as one of the best at spinning tall yarns. He told of a petrified forest where petrified birds sat on petrified limbs and sang petrified songs while petrified flowers bloomed below.

With a twinkle in his eye, the husky, bushy-bearded trapper also told of an amazing lake he knew about. He said there was a boiling-

Many of the "tall tales" told by mountain men were really true stories about hot springs and geysers in the Yellowstone country.

hot spring at the edge of the lake. When he caught a trout, all he had to do was to pull it in through the spring to have the fish cooked by the time it came to him. When his friends hooted at that one, Jim went on to tell them about a swift river that was hot on the bottom from rushing so fast over rocks.

One of Jim's most famous stories was about an "alarm clock" echo. He told the tale to show how big the wilderness was.

"When this ol' hoss turned in fer the night," Jim would say with a straight face, "all he had to do was yell 'Time to git up!' Bless me if eight hours later that echo didn't come to rouse him out of his sleep!"

Good-natured Joe Meek was another great storyteller. A greenhorn once asked him if he'd seen many changes come to the West. Joe had a quick answer. "I shorely have," he said. "Why, when I first come out here, Mount Hood, which is the highest mountain in the Oregon Country, warn't nothin' but a hole in the ground!"

Not all of the stories were made up. Jim Bridger once told one that no one believed for a while. But it was true. He said he had floated down the swift Bear River in a round

boat made of buffalo hides stretched on a
frame of willow boughs. It was a wild ride
through steep-walled canyons. He came at last
to a huge body of water. Jim leaned over for
a drink. The water was so salty he spit it out.
Jim thought he had come to the Pacific Ocean.
Other trappers howled with laughter at what
they took to be another of Jim's tall tales. But
the truth was that Bridger had discovered the
Great Salt Lake in what is now Utah.

But it was not always peaceful and jolly in the winter lodges. Sometimes hostile Indians would sneak up to steal horses from the pens. If the mountain men discovered the raid in time, they would snatch up their guns and rush out to beat off the Indians. But if the horses had already been stolen, the mountain men would make a chase to get back their animals. The Indians were good at hiding their trail—unless they had Kit Carson after them. He was the best tracker in the mountains, better than any Indian. The stubborn little man once tracked a band of horse thieves for three hundred miles to get back the animals that belonged to him.

Tall tales, battles, chases—they all helped to make time pass faster until spring and the beginning of another trapping season. Then the men would start storing up furs to take to the annual rendezvous.

8. The Mountain Carnival

Old Pete nudged the young man in the ribs. "Well, thar it is," Pete said, pointing down at the wide, green valley. "Your first look at a rendezvous! What do you think, Tom?"

Tom didn't know what to think. The scene below was as confusing as anything he'd ever seen. At least a thousand tepees stretched for miles along the creek that wound through the valley. The tepees were set up in groups, with space between to give the livestock plenty of grazing room. Trappers and Indians moved around as if stirred with a big stick. Laughing

80

Trappers greet each other in a painting of a Green
River Valley rendezvous by W. H. Jackson.

Indian children raced in and out. The noise
was terrific. Trappers shouted. Indians jab-
bered. Dogs yipped. Horses whinnied. Guns
were fired playfully into the air.

"When do things settle down?" young Tom
asked.

"Never! That's rendezvous for ye," Pete
replied. "Always somethin' doin'. It's what a
mountain man looks forward to from one year
to the next. He'll ride a thousand miles to
git to the chosen valley, and he'll git there
right smack on the time chosen for it. Well,
let's git down thar."

Old Pete, Tom, and a dozen other trappers led their horses and pack mules down into the valley.

This valley had been chosen at last year's rendezvous as the place for this year's meeting. All the trappers in the mountains knew about it. The time was early July, when most rendezvous were held. Then the mountain passes were free of snow. The traders from St. Louis could bring in their pack trains without much trouble. Also, as the beaver were shedding in summer, they were not worth trapping.

As Tom and his fellows trudged along the line of tepees, trappers shouted greetings and Tom's friends roared back.

"Hey, Pete!" someone sitting by a campfire yelled. "I thought fer sure the Blackfeet would have lifted your hair by now."

"Not mine," Pete replied. "I took care of that myself." He whipped off his hat and showed a head that was naturally bald. The trappers slapped their legs and hooted with laughter.

A few of their Indian wives giggled without understanding the joke. Trappers were proud of their wives and wanted them to outshine all other squaws. So these women wore dresses of the softest buckskin. Their moccasins were trimmed with porcupine quills in many colors. They wore bright, silk scarves and colorful beads around their necks. Ribbons or combs were in their braided hair.

Tom and his friends set up their tents by the stream. This would be their headquarters while they were at the rendezvous. But they would spend much of their time visiting around the huge camp, eating and drinking with all of their friends.

Mountain men wanted to have fun at the

rendezvous but business came first. Tom's group took its bales of fur to the traders' tents that were set up at a central place. There a price per skin was agreed upon. But before the businessmen from the East paid for the furs, they checked their record books. Many of the mountain men owed money for supplies that they had bought the year before. This debt was taken from their accounts. Then, when the trappers knew exactly how much money was coming to them, they bought what they would need for the coming year.

Tom was amazed at the high prices they were charged. A pound of coffee or sugar cost as much as four dollars. He saw many things spread out on the traders' blankets that cost many times as much here as they would cost in St. Louis. Of course, the traders had had to come a long way and to take risks. But Tom was beginning to see why mountain men never made the fortunes they hoped for. He doubted many of them ever got out of debt.

Yet supplies and new equipment were needed. The men needed powder, tobacco, hunting knives, traps, flints. They wanted thread, small tools, cooking kettles, and luxuries like flour, raisins, and dried fruit. Some of them also wanted things for their Indian wives. For them they bought beads, hand mirrors, bright cloth for skirts and scarves, small bells to sew to their moccasins, and paint for their faces.

Tom left Pete and his friends bargaining for supplies and wandered off by himself. His eyes feasted on the excitement. There was activity everywhere. He saw contests of all sorts going on. There were wrestling matches, footraces, weight-lifting contests, shooting matches, and horse races around a distant stake stuck in the ground. Indians, who came

to the rendezvous because of the fun, took part
in many of the games.

And always there was gambling on the
events. Mountain men loved to gamble. All
through the big camp Tom saw trappers
gambling on blankets with dice and cards.
They bet, too, on "hands," an Indian game.
The player passed a small bone or stone back
and forth from one hand to the other. His
hands moved swiftly. Others had to guess
which hand held the bone.

But not everything at the rendezvous was
good-natured fun. There were always bullies
in such a group of rugged men. They looked

for trouble and usually found it. Fights with fists, knives, or guns broke out. These were men who lived with violence every day.

Once a fight was over, it was forgotten. The men went back to their sport and fun.

As the days passed, Tom was amazed that the trappers could keep it up. The wild carnival went on day after day, lasting far into the night. The trappers loved to dance. They liked the slow, shuffling step of the Indians to the throbbing beat of drums. But they also liked to dance the reel, sometimes with each other, sometimes with giggling squaws.

After several days, Tom was exhausted just from watching all of the drinking, dancing, fighting, cavorting, and general commotion. He was almost glad when the traders had all the furs and the trappers had spent all their money. Then it was time to choose the place for next year's rendezvous. The traders headed back to St. Louis and the mountain men set out for the beaver streams. The fall trapping would soon begin.

9. The End of the Trade

In the early 1830's something happened in Europe that was to affect mountain men half a world away. Men began to wear tall hats made of silk. After a while this style spread to cities in the United States. The trappers did not know about this at first. All they knew was that the price of beaver fur kept going down. Soon they were getting no more than a dollar a pelt. This was hardly worth the time and trouble it took to trap for beaver. By 1840 the beaver trade was through.

Some of the mountain men refused to admit this. They kept on trapping but with no hope of making money at it. They did it because it was a way of life they loved, and because they hated to leave their beloved mountains.

Others soon faced the facts. Some of these returned to the settlements to earn a living. Some found new ways to support themselves in the Far West. Jim Bridger, for one, saw the growing tide of westward-moving settlers. He built a fort and trading post on the Oregon Trail in what is today southwest Wyoming to take care of the wagon trains. Other trappers found work as guides for the trains. Still

These buffalo hunters stretching hides in a camp on the plains, once trapped beaver in the Rockies.

Kit Carson became a guide and then an army officer in the War Between the States.

others became meat hunters for such places as Bent's Fort, or they hunted buffalo and sold the skins for robes. Then there were those who put all they had learned about the mountains to good use. They served as scouts for the army. But no matter how a trapper earned his living, he remained a proud mountain man for the rest of his life.

The mountain men had never stayed in one place long enough to help build towns or villages. Their years of greatness were few. But it would be hard to find a group that did more for the growth of America. Settlers traveled on trails that had been blazed by mountain men. Wagons rumbled through the mountain passes discovered by the trappers. They also found lakes and rivers, mighty peaks, and rich valleys that had not been seen before by white men. They were the first men to explore the wonders of the Yellowstone country. They, who were in the Far West first, played a big part in making it a part of the United States of America.

We will never know the names of most of these men who lived and worked in the wilderness when America was young. We only know the debt we owe them.

They were, by thunder, MOUNTAIN MEN!

Glossary

bandanna: a large, usually blue or red, patterned handkerchief

beaver "medicine": a mixture of beaver glands and herbs used as bait to attract beaver to traps

boss: the hump on the back of a buffalo's neck

breechclout: a cloth worn by the trappers in warm weather instead of trousers

buckskins: leather clothing made from the skins of sheep and deer

cache: a hole in the ground in which mountain men hid furs

capote: a long, hooded cloak

cavvy: a herd of extra animals following a wagon train

cold camp: a camp which had no campfire, where trappers slept without fear of attack

counting coup: this expression was used by Indians for daring acts of bravery

geyser: a spring which shoots streams of steam and boiling water into the air from time to time

greenhorn: a man who was new to the West, especially one who was not hardened to frontier life

hobble: to fasten the legs of an animal together so that it will not stray

jerky: meat which has been cut into long strips and dried in the sun

keelboat: a shallow river boat used by traders to carry furs and supplies

leggings: coverings for the legs, usually made of cloth or leather

mess: group of trappers who ate together in camp

pelt: the skin of a fur-bearing animal

pommel: the knob at the front of a saddle which bulges forward

possibles sack: a leather bag of things a mountain man might need in the wilderness

prairie schooners: the covered wagons which carried traders and settlers westward

ramrod: a rod used for ramming a charge into the muzzle of a firearm

rawhide: cattle skin which has not been made into leather

reel: a lively dance

rendezvous: the yearly meeting at which trappers, traders, and Indians swapped furs for goods

"Rocky Mountain College": the expression used by mountain men for the education they got from old books and trappers' tales

roster: a list of names

tethers: lines used for hitching or leading animals

thong: a strip of leather used as a rein or a fastener

traplines: a line or series of traps set by mountain men

venison: the edible flesh of a wild animal, especially a deer

Index